Create Me A Better Me
(A Conversation About Self-Transformation)

Create Me A Better ME
A Conversation About Self-Transformation

Create Me A Better Me
(A Conversation About Self-Transformation)

Create Me A Better ME
A Conversation About Self-Transformation

Floyd Boykin Jr.

SpokenVizions Publishing
SpokenVizions Entertainment Group, LLC

Create Me A Better Me
(A Conversation About Self-Transformation)

Create Me A Better Me
A Conversation About Self-Transformation
by Floyd Boykin Jr.

Published by SpokenVizions Entertainment Group, LLC.
This book is available at http://www.spokenvizions.com

Edited by Safiyyah Amina
Cover design: Floyd Boykin Jr.
Type design and typography: Floyd Boykin Jr.

Copyright © 2014 by Floyd Boykin Jr.
http://www.floydboykinjr.com

ISBN 0-9773834-7-4

This book is subject to the conditions that it shall not, by way of trade or otherwise, be lent, re-sold, hired out, or otherwise circulated without the publisher's prior consent in any form of binding or cover other than that in which it is published and without a similar condition being imposed on the subsequent purchaser.

All rights reserved. No part of this publication may be produced, stored in a retrieval system, or transmitted, in any form or by any means, electronic, mechanical, photocopying, recording, or otherwise, without prior permission of the publisher.

Published 2014

About the Author

This is the first Self-Help/Motivational book from magazine editor, motivational speaker, published poet, songwriter, Lupus awareness advocate, musician, recording artist, and film producer Floyd Boykin Jr. Mr. Boykin is the creator, editor and founder of the 3x award winning publication SpokenVizions Magazine. It is a publication that is geared towards the accomplishments and lifestyles of spoken word poets through out the country. He has a bachelor's degree in Speech Communications and Theaters Arts from Monmouth College in Illinois. Boykin has three published poetry books, four spoken word poetry music albums, and he is also the creator of his own greeting card line called "PoeticByDesign."

Boykin first began performing poetry in 1997 at a spoken word venue in St. Louis, Missouri called Club Divinity, which eventually landed him the opportunity to open up for the legendary group The Last Poets. Floyd has also opened for the legendary Gil Scott-Heron, Malik Yusef, and neo-soul singer Goapele, amongst others. He has won and placed in several spoken word poetry slams, created a lupus benefit concert called "Poets Against Lupus" and he has also perform in several benefit programs.

Create Me A Better Me
(A Conversation About Self-Transformation)

CONTENTS

<u>Acknowledgement</u>   xi

<u>Introduction</u>   xiv

<u>Chapter 1</u>
Don't Stay The SAME AND COMPLAIN   1

<u>CHAPTER 2</u>
GET NAKED   4

<u>CHAPTER 3</u>
THE THREE KEYS TO TRANSFORMATION   6

<u>CHAPTER 4</u>
THE RE-FACTOR   14

<u>CHAPTER 5</u>
CLEARING A PATH FOR GREATNESS   16

<u>CHAPTER 6</u>
HARD NOT IMPOSSIBLE (THE DITCH STATUS)   20

Create Me A Better Me
(A conversation about self-transformation)

Chapter 7
12 POWER WORDS TO BUILD CHARACTER   25

CHAPTER 8
COMMIT TO YOURSELF   31

CHAPTER 9
LANGUAGE MATTERS   34

CHAPTER 10
YOUR GREETINGS SAYS A LOT ABOUT YOU   38

CHAPTER 11
BEWARE OF THE BUZZ KILLER   46

CHAPTER 12
FORGIVING YOURSELF   53

CHAPTER 13
DRESS TO FEEL GOOD; DRESS TO EMPOWER   56

CHAPTER 14
REACT BY NOT REACTING   60

Create Me A Better Me
(A conversation about self-transformation)

Chapter 15
THE FIVE DEADLY WORD VENOMS OF SELF-DEFEAT   63

CHAPTER 16
SET THE TONE FOR THE WEEK   68

CHAPTER 17
LIFE IS FULL OF POSSIBILITIES   72

RECOMMENDED READINGS   75

RECOMMENDED MUSICAL PROJECTS   76

EMPOWERMENT MOVEMENT   77

INDEX   78

ACKNOWLEDGMENT

I am totally grateful to each and every one who has encouraged and supported the concept and vision of this project. All of you are very key in providing me with the focus to complete these thoughts. Also, I want to thank all of the people who sent me random e-mails, inbox messages on Facebook and YouTube, Tweets on Twitter, or who simply contacted me the old fashioned way, by phone, to express to me that the work that I do with my music, my poetry, my videos and my publications have inspired your lives or helped you think about a subject differently based on my words. Words truly have power. I would like to, particularly, thank my beloved wife Jacquette and my brilliant son Floyd (FB3) Grace Chung, Kimeko Farrar, Selena J, Venus Jones, Ron Williams, Keya McClain-Harris, Quashana Foster-Spaulding, Venencia Danielle Small, Tantra-Zawadi, Alice Blaylock Pitts, Safiyyah Amina Muhammad, Jessica McCaskill, Saidia Murphy, my cousins (Tracy Mitchell, Al Caldwell, Islandia Whidbee, Cynthia Hopson, Erica and Robert Lewis, Kimberly Renea), my brother Kahsan and my father (Floyd Sr.) for his incredible support and belief in me and the gifts that God has bestowed upon me. Also, I send blessings to the memory of my extraordinary mother (Gloria H. Boykin) who passed away in 1993 due to complications from Lupus. Thank you for your guidance and for setting me on a great path in life. Because of all of your encouragement and beliefs that I could even write a book of this nature; it pushes me to levels that I didn't think I had in me.

I thank you for being by my side regardless of what's going on in your lives. I give many thanks for my wonderful staffers at SpokenVizions Magazine. You all are the greatest. The energy that I have gotten from the constant hours of networking face to face and on social sites has fueled a part of me that I didn't see 5 years ago. I am forever on the journey of transformation.

Introduction

This is the first Self-Help/Motivational book I've written. I published three poetry books; *"Poetic Bliss with Lyrical Rhythms"*, *"Bare Essence: The Soul of Me"* and *"Waiting to Dance with Her Spirit"*. And, I also released four poetry musical projects; *"Planet Liberation"*, *"EKLIPSE"*, *"EARTHOLOGY"* and *"W.A.R. on RedMoon7"*. The concept of this book came from three sources. On my album *"W.A.R. on RedMoon7"*, I wrote a song, along with singer InnaRae called *"Create Me a Better Me"*, thus the title of this book. Also, as editor and founder of SpokenVizions Magazine, I have published over 30 issues. I have a page that is a staple in the publication called "From Within". It is my editorial page, highly inspired by the former editor of Essence Magazine, Susan Taylor. I have received countless e-mails about the inspiring messages and the energy of that page. I have often expressed to people that one of my primary functions as a writer is to inspire; so I am very proud of that section of the magazine. The third event was my personal journey with weight loss, spiritual and emotional relief and the longing feeling of wanting to be a great example for my one and only child, Floyd Boykin III (Tre or FB3). It seems as if this book was writing itself right in front of my very eyes and, therefore, it was pretty natural to write about transforming myself into a better me. The title *"Create Me a Better Me"* was born as I was listening to *"Seattle"* by gospel duo Mary Mary. That song changed my life, so I wanted to share my thoughts and experiences with you in book form. If after reading this book you are inspired to take the next level in your life to be a better person, my mission is accomplished. We are all jewels tapping into the power that we all possess inside to be extraordinary people. I wrote this book as if I was talking to several of my closest friends. So, consider yourself a friend and let's start the journey!!!!

Chapter 1
DON'T STAY THE SAME AND COMPLAIN

This book is a great book to spark conversation about improving oneself. It's not a doctoral offering or a psychiatrist offering. It is a young educated artist seeking transformation in oneself.

There comes a time when you have to ask yourself a very serious question; and if you are reading this book, the time is now. That question is, "Do you really want to change?" Or better yet, "Are you ready to commit to yourself in order to change?" Many of us, including myself, have fallen into this category of "acceptance and complacency". We complain as much as we can and to whom ever will listen to our problems, without any solutions or attempts to make things better for self. It's as if we have this built in perpetual venting mechanism implanted within us. Don't get me wrong, venting is good to a degree because it's a way to expel certain energies out of our system, but it's my belief that venting has an expiration date and we MUST enforce that. If we don't, we are technically making ourselves mentally ill, therefore emotionally and spiritually ill, which will continue to manifest a physical illness caused by stress.

When people say "Well, this is just who I am. I ain't never gonna change"; I believe them. You know why? I believe it because they believe it. But the truth is that I despise that statement because a person gives up before trying. It shows stubbornness that is a hindrance. To a degree, it's a cop out because you justify your current condition and disposition to maintain a sense of normalcy. A person who isn't willing to grow will slowly decay until they become a walking programmed zombie living in a world that was created by self. We can change if we choose to do so.

As long as we continue to complain about the exact same things in our lives, over and over and over again, we create a permanent emotional tenant that lives with us rent free. This book is meant to help us become better emotional and spiritual landlords so that we can get our houses in order. People will say that this is easier said than done.

Well, no one said that it was going to be easy and besides, isn't the peace of your mind and the calming of your spirit worth trying? Just a thought, but I know it was for me. Too many times we give up on ourselves because we claim it's too hard to transform, when in essence, what we are really saying is that it's easier to stay the same and complain. Those were the subtitles that came across my screen (my eyes) when I continued seeing people convincing themselves that putting in the work to create "a better you" is too difficult. If you are choosing not to do the work, find it in your heart to shut your mouth about the situation. But if you are ready to move forward, and I mean honestly ready to move forward, then let's open that conversation up. Do the work, believe in yourself and make it happen. Don't stay the same and complain. It's very toxic and it's not productive for the growth of a better you. Clear out your emotional, mental, and spiritual closets. Transformation can only take place when you create space for it. Well, if you are ready, then take a journey with me starting now.

Chapter 2

Get Naked

Get Naked. What a way to start off a chapter of a motivational book. When I say "Get Naked", I mean it in a psychological, spiritual, and emotional manner. This is a motivational book about transforming our thoughts, our image of self, and tapping into our purpose in life. It's an opportunity for us to access our current situation, reshape our self-esteem and create a space within our universe where we can live in harmony with the thing or things that we are most passionate about. Many times, so many things or circumstances happen in our day to day lives that we lose sight of our true selves. Our purpose in life is to create and live in love, yet we are often derailed from that path and become stagnant in complacency with comfortable environments where we just adapt, adjust and assimilate. We lose ourselves into society and unfortunately betray our hearts, therefore we betray ourselves.

Getting naked allows us to strip down all of our emotional, spiritual and psychological baggage so that we can become vulnerable and transparent. It's the same concept of an effective spoken word poetry performance. When a poet performs, the objective often is to teleport the soul or the spirit of all who are listening back to the very conception of the piece. Poets have to be so passionate about the presentation of the poem, that you as the audience feel like you experienced the situation along with that poet. In order to be effective like this, the poet subconsciously stripped down to his or her vulnerable spiritual self and then began the journey. This is what we have to do to ourselves in order to effectively transform ourselves. Ironically, our audience for this life presentation is ourselves. We have to step outside of ourselves and lay eyes on that which we are trying to change so that we can determine the path of self and live in love. Some may refer to this as an out of body experience or even call it a spiritual enlightenment; or as Oprah often says, an "ah ha moment", if you will. It is at this moment we make a conscious decision about transforming our lives; our being into something greater. It is at this very moment that we have a conversation with self and we tell ourselves that we know that there is a greater experience in life that awaits us. This must happen. The only way any conscious change is going to happen is that we must first acknowledge that a change needs to take place. We then must change our insides to transform the outside.

Once we transform ourselves and create a space for us, our purpose emerges. It's very hard to see purpose through clutter and confusion. It's very hard to experience love for ourselves when our surroundings are not filled with love. Are you willing to get naked so that you can introduce yourself to the new you? Are you ready to be the "you" you were meant to be? Then let's get naked.

Chapter 3

The 3 Keys to Transformation

Healing your thoughts:

You are NOT a victim. Once you eliminate that label from your consciousness, you will begin your path towards mental freedom. I read a quote that paraphrased, stated, "If you want to change your life, then change the way you think." I find that to be so true because many of us are imprisoned by our own thoughts. We have so many concepts and ideologies that were passed on to us by our parents, our churches, our family, our friends, or just misconceptions based on misinformation. This is very debilitating, which causes us not to grow. It causes us to turn our backs on the natural progression of self, based on fear, ignorance and the misconception that "there's nothing wrong with me" syndrome; self-denial that the way we look at things could be incorrect. I believe its arrogance and foolishness that keeps us bounded to our current self. Face it y'all, the old way of thinking is not working; if they were, you wouldn't even give this book a second thought. There's something about the concept of creating a better you that compelled you to pick up this book or any motivational book. So let's start transforming ourselves beginning with the mind, because after all, when the mind and head lead, the rest will follow. It is essential that we change the way we think to have the ability and the desire to transform ourselves. There are three things to think about in your transformation of your thought process. I call them *The Three Keys to Transformation*. The Three Keys to Transformation consist of Acknowledgment, Empowerment and Excitement, also known as the AEE Method.

The Three Keys to Transformation:
Acknowledgment, Empowerment and Excitement.

Acknowledgment: Saying to yourself, or out loud, "I want to make a better me", is a major statement. That means that you are willing to enhance yourself in all aspects of your life; such as your personal life, home life, your marriage or relationship, parenthood, your religion or faith, as a man or woman, in finances, as an artist, or a business man. Confessing out loud or to the universe that you are ready to make a change is the first and possibly the biggest step. You must speak it into existence. Speak it, believe it and mean it; because if you are not whole heartedly ready to transform, you will not see any results. You have to work to make this happen for you. Faith without works is dead. Isn't that what The Good Book says? Be very serious. Acknowledge your good attributes, as well as things that you need to work on. In this stage, you acknowledge that whatever you have been doing in the past hasn't really been working that well for you. You find yourself in the "same ole" routine of immobility and no purpose day after day. You acknowledge that you are ready to find your person, your passion and your purpose.

Say, "I want to be a better me", out loud and be ready for it. By putting it out into the universe, you are sending signals or a message that will come back as energy to assist you. You will start getting information that will help you along the way to achieve your transformation. You will start meeting people who can help you on your journey. People will start recommending books to you that seem to be actually what you needed at the time. It's amazing what comes your way when you are ready to receive it. This will lead you to the next stage, which is empowerment.

Empowerment: Once you start receiving information that will enlighten, educate or make you aware of steps leading you forward on your journey, you begin to feel empowered. You feel like the universe, or God, is confirming what you need to achieve your goal of transformation. What you put out to the universe will come back to you. It is genuine energy. It was a genuine feeling, so you "willed" the information to you. It's the Law of Attraction. You put out genuine energy about something and God/The Universe will supply you with what you need to achieve what you have set out to do.

Excitement: The third key is very simple. After you acknowledge a need for change, make moves to achieve these changes which empower you; you become excited! Excitement is what keeps you on the path to a better you. If you aren't excited about transformation, or anything else for that matter, your interest level will deplete and ultimately you will abandon the journey. Staying excited keeps you looking forward to the next chapter of a better you.

> *"Nothing new can come into your life unless you are grateful for what you already have."*
> -Dr. Michael Beckwith, The Secret.

When a person begins their journey into transformation, there are key elements that must take place to have a successful life session with the decision to improve or change. Yes, I said life session because once you decide to change, you will never be the same nor do you want to go back to the "days of ole". When you make a decision to improve your life, you also have to make the decision to maintain and continue to enhance that decision. It's a life change. Your life will begin to change in ways that you never imagined because previously your mind wasn't in a place that would allow the idea of change to populate your thoughts. More than likely, your mind and spirit were cluttered with mental, emotional, and spiritual baggage that consistently worked to block any blessings, or constant positive flow of energy into your life. And once you achieve one mission, it will open doors for the missions involving change.

First off, the key to changing your life is the realization that your life needs to have a change. Let's do some soul searching. What is it about ourselves that we would want to improve upon? We often place blame on others for the shortcomings of our lives. We have to own and accept the responsibility of our own lives. As Mahatma Ghandi stated,

"Be the change that you wish to see in the world." Don't say, "What's wrong with me?" Interrogating yourself initiates negative energy. Negative thinking lowers self-esteem and causes misdirection. Ask yourself instead, "How can I improve myself?" Words have power. LANGUAGE is very powerful. When we were children, people would say "Sticks and stones may break my bones but words will never hurt me." Then someone would maliciously say something that would destroy our character in front of people (that girl or guy you were trying to impress, your friends, etc) and you realize that words do hurt. They can hurt really badly depending on who may be using the words as weapons. But the great thing about words... they can also be used to heal, to improve, to manifest the awesomeness that we all process inside. Words are healers and guiders and we must use them responsibly.

------ Transition

We must change the way we think. Once we get a handle on our thoughts, we will notice that everything outside of our thoughts will start to change. So, as a person thinks, so he/she does.

The biggest change for me came when my mother passed away back in 1993 from complications with LUPUS. She was very depressed and just unhappy with life. Seeing my mother suffering gave me the drive to be greater than what I've seen in my life; greater than those "Kats" just hanging out on the corner. I didn't want to become what I saw my mother become. She was that woman who sat in her bedroom, with the lights off, rugs over the window so that no light could come in, a cigarette in one hand and a Budweiser beer in the other, frowning and complaining about life. We are only here for a short period of time and I want my time to really count. This may mean different things for different people.

I started working on my thinking by reading self help books and learning to think, speak and feel positively. It takes so much less energy to do this than to be that constant complainer or that crippling voice that's always knocking us down with doubt and disbelief. In order for us to achieve greatness or simply pursue the transformation of self, we have to first assess our situation. Once we assess or acknowledge that a change has to be made, it's easy to determine what those changes are. Then, we usually seek out material or even someone to talk to that can and will empower us with the knowledge and confidence to move forward in a greater light. This allows us to empower ourselves.

For example, I lost 26 pounds in the last $2^{1/2}$ months. I saw a video of myself. My stomach was a growing planet. I said, "GOD is that me? WOW! I truly need to lose some weight." That was me acknowledging that I had a gut and it was time to do something about it. I started seeking out information about healthier eating habits, exercise, sodium, protein and cholesterol intake. People starting supplying me with information, then I started my weight loss journey. I became EMPOWERED. I started losing weight gradually. I was so excited to see progress; I became even more dedicated to the cause. EXCITED! I'm the lightest I've been in 7 years. It feels great.

I absolutely love setting goals and getting them accomplished. But I didn't used to be like that. I used to be extremely shy, I had a speech problem, and I was very geeky. But the more I learned and the more I got into writing poetry, songs and music; I started to see a change in me and the way I affected so many people. It really made me want to do more for people. I used this same concept in terms of being the "Go Getter" that my poetic sister, Rose calls me. Surround yourself with positive people, positive activities, positive music, positive everything!

> *"We are all Super Heroes. Many of us just haven't tapped into our powers yet. Many of us just don't believe that we are powerful."*
>
> *-Floyd Boykin Jr.*

You can achieve greatness from your writings without being a major social butterfly. The internet allows you to do that. You don't have to be up in people's faces to get your material out; there are blogs, social media, etc. But if you are just writing for yourself, you can still do things as a home body to be a greater you, a happier you, if indeed that is what you want. You have to first claim it. You have to tell yourself, pray, mediate and confess out loud that you want to be a better you. All the right answers and the proper direction will come your way because you want them to genuinely appear. Seeing the power in my craft has continued to ignite my flame daily.

CREATE ME A BETTER ME AFFIRMATION

I am ready to experience the ultimate challenge.
I am extraordinary.
I am to live each day with meaning.
I am ready to live my life abundantly
to increase my wealth, physical, mental
and spiritual health.
I am ready to give freely of myself and
Open to receive graciously.
My spirit is humble, blessed and grateful.
I am grateful for all that I have and will have.
I am ready to give love, show love and
become love.
Respect myself most, so that I can respect
others more.
I am ready to… Create Me a Better Me.

by Floyd Boykin Jr.

This book wasn't created to replace faith, or as an alternative to spiritual or religious beliefs. It was created to assist those wanting to create a better being.

[Byrne, Rhonda. The Secret. (Atria Books, New York, 2006; Beyond Words, Oregon, 2006).]

Chapter 4

The RE-Factor

"Happiness is a journey and not a destination." This is a very personal quote by Ben Sweetland that I have adapted to my lifestyle. It's very important that I get you to understand this as well. Happiness is not in the hands of others unless you put it there. We are in control of the happiness in our lives. We have the power to maintain that happiness and to eliminate anything that is contradictory or adverse to that journey. In order to be on your way to transformation, you MUST look at the world through different eyes because, trust me, if things were the way we wanted them to be, I wouldn't have written this book and you would not be reading this book. But it's awesome that we are both open to the possibility of creating a better being; a better person.

Changing the way you think, changes the way you perceive life; therefore, it changes the way you live. Unfortunately and fortunately, it took the birth of my one and only son for me to start re-evaluating my thought process. It is because of my son that I started embracing life differently. I want to live. I want to be here for my son as much as I can and the only way that I can do that is by being here. I have to live better. I have to make better decisions about my health.

I have to make better financial decisions. I have to make better decisions on the type of food and beverages that I put into my body, as well as the amount of food and beverages that I put into my body. I have to get into physical shape and RE-shape my body, RE-shape my mind and RE-shape my spirit. I have to RE-condition my spirit to change my disposition.

Keep "Gratitude Journals". Learn to be grateful. Nothing new can come into your life unless you are grateful for what you already have. EVERY MORNING wake up and say: "I am thankful for my health. I am thankful for my limbs. I am thankful for my family. I chose today to give my life the best life ever."

Once you get your mind on track, you can't go back.

[Oprah Winfrey Show: The Secret. *Gratitude Journal).]

Chapter 5

Clearing a Path for Greatness

Ask yourself this question. Is it easier to get to the other side of a road with obstacles blocking the path, or is it easier to get to the other side of the road when it's completely clear? Your answer should be a clear path. Now apply that to your life in the mental, emotional, spiritual and physical sense. When there is clutter blocking or slowing up your energy, you tend to wear down easier or easily. Sometimes, you may even give up quickly because it seems as if the obstacles are just too overbearing for you at that time. How many times have you come home and your house wasn't clean and it seems like you instantly become drained because you know you are going to have to clean your house? You become stressed out and your thoughts become jumbled and you almost feel unorganized at the time. It is a natural feeling when objects (physical or emotional) sidetrack you from the important things in life. It takes you away from being organized. When you come home to a clean home, it's like a breath of fresh air. Your mind is free and clear, thoughts flow quickly and creatively, time is freed up to do something else on your agenda, and you are a little to a lot less stressed because you can chose to relax or do a project in the house if you want to. When you or your mind is cluttered, it takes away from other important things that you could be building on in your life. It is believed that if your life is "cluttered", it's hard for positive flow of energy to come your way, because you don't have any space for anything else. You have blocked your blessing, your path, based on clutter.

I'm sure you have heard of the phrase "Get your house in order." This is all common sense, but many times we wouldn't think about this type of thing unless someone brings it back up into our lives. Consider this as that moment. To aid me, I have read a lot on Feng Shui, recently a book by Karen Kingston called "Clear Your Clutter with Feng Shui."

I am a firm believer that clutter blocks the positive flow of energy. Part of mental clutter is not being grateful for the things you have in your life. When you start appreciating what you already own in your life, you allow space, time and room for new things to come into your life. When you are ungrateful, you become stagnant and you become your biggest obstacle. A major part of transformation is changing the way we think about things. Let me give you an example. I am a musician, as well as a poet. I create often, but sometimes, my writing is blocked for one reason or another. Well, I decided to clean up my messy studio office that I happened to have let get cluttered up for weeks. We all get busy and sometimes cleaning isn't at the top of the list, at least not for most guys. Of course I'm generalizing. But once I cleaned up my office and also put up my vision board (An organizational tool that I use to bring focus into my life; which I will discuss in a later chapter) I became swamped with highly creative ideas. I started writing music, and poems. I started writing parts of this book. I became so overcharged that my mind felt like it was on the verge of exploding, with parts of my thoughts falling all over the ground. It was amazing. My cousin, Robert, was having the same issue, so I told him what I did; the whole clearing clutter concept. Within days, he contacted me and told me that out of nowhere, he was writing and doing music again. He stated that he did what I told him to do and cleaned up his space. He cleaned up his clutter to allow creative energy back into his space.

Like pre-school and elementary teachers do for their students when they are behaving poorly, or if they are whining or crying about something, they redirect their attention to something else to produce happiness, contentment or focus on something else. The same method works on adults. If you find yourself thinking negatively, call up a positive thinking friend, or read a book. Go over to that brand new space that you have cleaned up and pray, meditate or do whatever you do to connect with God, The Creator, The Higher Power or whatever power or term you use to address your belief and faith. Make this habitual or routine and you will start seeing that those negative thoughts no longer have a home in your mind. Negative people no longer have a home in your space. Negative things no longer have a home in your universe. Now you can't stop negativity from existing and showing up in your lives. That would not be realistic. But you can control the majority of the flow of positive energy that you project in your life and in your mind. I guarantee, if you do this, it will decrease the flow of negative energy tremendously. Sometimes it will include not talking to certain friends and family to achieve it. It doesn't mean that you don't love them; it just means that you have identified that these individuals bring drama and unwanted elements into your life that stress you out or causes you to look at things in a negative light. This book is about transforming YOU, not the people around you. But you have to focus on you before you can proactively help someone else. They may see the change in your life and want to know what's going on with you. I get asked questions every day from people trying to figure out what I'm "up to" because I'm always happy, smiling, and feeling extraordinary. I tell them I'm up to living my life in wonderful peace.

[Kingston, Karen. *Clear Your Clutter with Feng Shui: Free Yourself from Physical, Mental, Emotional, and Spiritual Clutter Forever.* (Piatkus, UK, 1998; Broadway Books, New York, 1999).]

Chapter 6
Hard Not Impossible
(The Ditch Status)

"Use your words to bless your future not curse your future."
-Pastor Joel Osteen

Hard and difficult do not mean impossible. But when your mind is coded with a shield of negative energy based on personal experiences and tainted thoughts, it doesn't feel achievable. I'm here to tell you that it is indeed achievable. Many people are more pessimistic that they are willing to admit. People will ask for advice or ask for your opinion to "help" them with their situation, but they will spend the majority of the time defending their negative thoughts. They will constantly ask questions to try and maintain their situation in a "ditch status". **A Ditch Status** is when you commit yourself to negative thoughts and actions to the degree that you will defend that behavior regardless of the truths that are presented in front of you. Therefore, you remain in a contained ditch, unwilling to actually get out of it; but will complain about being in it. For example, an associate of mine stated to me, "I am so tired of being alone and meeting the same type of people. All they want is sex, or just wanna [sic] play games. I give my heart completely and they just run over me each and every time." I believe that we attract these situations to our lives by not doing the necessary things to divert that energy from our space. I told her, "Don't worry about being alone. Since you aren't having a lot of success right now in dating, perhaps you should focus on you. Do what you need to do to make sure that you are happy in your life. Get yourself together spiritually, emotionally and physically and then you will start attracting a different type of person to you because you would be a different and improved person yourself." She then went on to say "But what if I still attract the same person. I hate being alone. I would just wanna [sic] be with someone. I would rather be in a bad relationship than alone." I asked, "So instead of improving yourself, you would rather be in something that's unhealthy emotionally and spiritually, that will ultimately lead you back to being alone again?" "It's not that..." she argued, "... it's too hard to focus on all those things. I just want to be with someone." I said, "But if you take your mind off of being with someone so badly, you can focus on what you need to do to attract the right type of person that would stand a better chance of staying in your life and giving you what you feel you need in a relationship." She rebutted, "So, what if I get with the person you speak of and I mess it up? What if I'm not what he needs and wants?" This conversation continued down this path until I ultimately abandoned ship. You gotta know when to end a conversation. Anyway, my point is that, no matter what information she would have received to give her an option for a better dating scenario, she would shoot it down before trying, because she has convinced herself that it will never change, so why even try. She's in a Ditch Status.

In order to break the chains of the "DS", you HAVE to be willing to change your mentality. Change the way you think because if you don't do this, it doesn't matter what book you read, what people you speak to or council with, you will never rise above the obstacle of defeat that you facilitate for yourself daily.

I was listening to Pastor Joel Osteen give a sermon on power of the words "I Am". He said "Never speak negative words about yourself. Do not give those words life." He also stated that "Whatever follows 'I Am' will come looking for you." I started thinking about the conversation that I had with my associate and, based on these statements; it was quite clear to me that SHE is creating the world that she's in. She doesn't believe that she's worthy of anything other than what she's been experiencing. If she thought differently about herself, she would have a different story to tell.

> *"Your life is the way you see it. You become what you believe."*
> *- Oprah Winfrey*

In order to have a different experience on the outside, you must create a better world on the inside. So I created an "I Am" list that I use every day as a daily affirmation and confirmation on who I am. You can develop your own list, but review my list as a guide. Once you start using a list like this, you MUST believe in the words that you are saying. The "I Am's" that come out of your mouth will determine your success or your failure. Whatever follows "**I AM**", will come looking for you.

I AM…
Inspired by motivational speaker Joel Osteen

I AM **B**lessed
I AM **W**orthy
I AM **H**ealthy
I AM **B**eautiful
I AM **Y**outhful
I AM **T**alented
I AM **C**reative
I AM **A**mazing
I AM a **M**asterpiece
I AM **E**xtraordinary
I AM **S**uccessful
I AM **V**aluable
I AM **S**exy
I AM **A**ttractive
I AM **P**eaceful
I AM **U**nique
I AM **C**onfident
I AM **S**trong
I AM **F**inancially **A**ble
I AM **I**ntelligent
I AM **E**mpowered
I AM **A**nointed
I AM **L**ove
I AM **F**earless
I AM a **V**isionary
I AM **V**ictorious
I AM **E**nergized
I AM **P**ositive

I AM **R**enewed
I AM **H**appy
I AM **S**piritually **G**rowing
I AM **F**illed **W**ith **W**isdom
I AM a **G**ood **L**earner
I AM a **G**ood **S**tudent
I AM a **G**ood **T**eacher
I AM **Q**ualified
I AM **E**ducated
I AM **G**ifted
I AM **B**rilliant
I AM **H**umble
I AM **E**ncouraged
I AM **I**nnovative
I AM **P**owerful
I AM **I**nspired

by Floyd Boykin Jr. © 05.15.2013

Chapter 7

12 Power Words to Enhance Character

"Create Me A Better Me" is a book about learning how to love yourself and executing that love in the universe to produce more love. In my journey of transforming myself into what I would call a better person, a better human being, I have come to embrace certain words that I believe are essential in shaping or molding one's character. Of course these words are not the only words that are deemed strong or worthy of creating a being of substance; but for me, they are a must have in maintaining a healthy mental state of being and a great positive aspect of life. These words do not come in any specific order, but they have helped ME to have ORDER within my life. These are my **12 Power Words to Enhance Character.**

Purpose: A major question that many people ask themselves is *"What is my purpose?"* Purpose is essential in our lives. It's the very reason why we live and do what we do. Determine your purpose. This could be done through meditation or praying to God and asking for guidance or signs to lead you to your purpose. If you find yourself having a certain passion for something such as music, inspiring people, a love for growing food, cooking, or anything that consumes your mind non-stop, do not ignore it. It could be the first strong sign to help you to decide what your purpose is.

Love: Love is the main ingredient in transformation. It is the one thing that will influence the majority of your journey. Without love, you have no desire to be a better person, or a respectful person. You would not care about any kind of vision and integrity would be a joke. Love is when you genuinely are concerned about your brothers and sisters of humanity. It's a deeper affection that will guide your decisions in life subconsciously and consciously. When you have developed an extraordinary love for yourself, the world will benefit from the energy that you place into action. Love is the theme music to everything. And if you believe that love is God and God is love, why would you not want love to consume your heart and be of love yourself; because, to be of love means to be of God.

Believe: In building self-esteem, developing love, or achieving dreams, the one thing that you MUST do is BELIEVE in yourself and the task at hand. If you do not believe in yourself, you can't expect someone else to. The belief begins with you. Trust me, when you believe in what you do and who you are, or what you stand for, others will notice and it will cause a domino effect of people who support, love and believe in you as well.

Focus: I found in my journey that becoming focused on the things that I desire, such as mental health, weight loss and weight control, love, happiness, and many other aspects of my life, was so very important. I actually created a Vision Board to help with this process. A vision board is a great tool to help you develop a central point in and of your life. A Vision Board is usually a foam platform where you organize photos and words in a central location to organize goals and aspirations. You hang it up in a location that you will see every day so that it stays in the forefront of your mind. We all have dreams, but many times, if they are not right in our faces every day, they will be placed on the back-burner of our lives stamped "Life Happens." This is just one way to help you get focused. It has helped me in many ways. I also meditate in the morning to clear my mind so that I can focus on the day and release stress. Get focused, accomplish your dreams. *WHATEVER WE GIVE OUR ATTENTION TO CONTROLS OUR ENERGY. Thoughts and feelings control our energy. What you focus on expands you. We create feelings through the books we read, the TV we view, the food we eat and the people we are around. Focus is about the feelings that the thoughts create.

Confident: As a performing artist, confidence is very important in delivering your message in a performance. You have to own it. Become the "art" to the point where the people who see you feel as if they were with you when you lived the experience that you wrote about. That is how we should live our lives... with confidence and with humility.
Anyone will tell you that a confident person is an attractive character of an ideal mate. It is very clear that people who are very sure of themselves, minus any trace of arrogance, are highly desirable. You feel you can trust them because of their certainty of their abilities. Your words and energy are much more believable when you convey them in a confident manner. Plus, confidence will make you do a much better

job at anything that you do, including being a better person.

Integrity: Integrity is what keeps you spiritually and morally grounded. It is important to us that we are quality people with words and action of substance. We have to do what we say we are going to do and honor that. Morality sets in and our belief system will help guide us and keep us on the right path. Also, anything that we are involved with, we genuinely want it to be the best we can offer people, or offer to ourselves. Integrity keeps us honest and valuable to many because people know that you will be about what you say you will do.

Courage: We face many things in our lives and sometimes we don't know if we have the energy to face them. Courage is that energy staring adversity directly in the face saying "I can do anything." Courage is the strength of your inner being that is determined to move forward regardless of the outcome. Courage partners up with the words and action of belief, because if you believe in something, you will have the courage to stand up for it, defend it, protect it, and love it, no matter what.

Resilient: Sometimes, even though we may know deep in our hearts that we are on the right path or doing something correctly, we face obstacles. Those obstacles may set us back but we MUST BE RESILIENT. We must bounce back and keep moving forward.

Respect: It is powerful when others hold you in high regards based on your character. To have a quality that people deem worthy of excellence is amazing and it's something that we work on every day. I have learned that we all have different beliefs and no one person is better than another. Respecting someone for who they are, their culture, family values, etc., is very key in connecting with others. I give respect regardless of whether you have earned it first because I try to treat people the way I want them to treat me.

Vision: "Without visions the people will perish." (Proverbs 29:18) For me, vision has always been a word and action that guides my life and my creativity. Often ideas come while I am sleeping. It is what breathes life into me. Having insight of what could come to pass is a beautiful way of creating a better you. Without a vision of how your life can and will be, where is the drive to create it.

Empower: It is my belief that we give ourselves authority to create our own world within our own universe. By learning, listening and being open to new ways of thinking empowers us daily. The thirst for knowledge gives us the strength to make our journey with happiness possible. By empowering ourselves, we empower others. We create freedom warriors to become better people, freeing our minds in the battle of a better we.

Create: We are all here to create and build. We are creative beings designed to mentally evolve so that we can reinvent what has manifested in our minds. Our job is to use that energy in a positive light and to ignite the flames in others. We create to inspire as we inspire to create. There is inspiration in everything we lay our eyes on. We just have to tap into our individual powers to enjoy or utilize it. This word and action lets me know that, mentally, "I have no boundaries and what I do to improve me through my ideas, could help or heal another". Through creating, my possibilities in life to do more are limitless.

All of these words helped to create and develop a stronger sense of humility, gratefulness, more positive thinking, increased wisdom, stronger self-esteem, and a greater love and appreciation of others, as well as myself. It has helped me to become the extraordinary person that I am. We all are extraordinary people. Unfortunately, some of us take the extra from the ordinary and become content with this, but we are all incredibly blessed individuals waiting to tap deeper into our spirits to become the people we were meant to be.

*[Byrne, Rhonda. The Secret. (Atria Books, New York, 2006; Beyond Words, Oregon, 2006).]

Chapter 8
Commit To Yourself

It is so easy for someone to just give up on themselves. That is the easy way out. There's no work to do. Just give in to whatever it is you were fighting; weight, impatience, profanity, spiritual beliefs, eating habits, exercise, love for someone and love for self, etc. But why not challenge yourself. If you don't like how things are in a certain situation, then change the way you think about it, process it and just do it. Will it be easy? Probably not, but the more you challenge yourself, the easier it will be. Ultimately it will become a positive lifestyle change for you. Whatever the case, just do it. You owe it to yourself to be the best person you can be. You are deserving of greatness. And if you do not think so, I am truly elated that you are reading this book, because you MUST rebuild and restructure your self-esteem so that you can see your self-worth. You are worthy to be loved by YOU. Without committing to yourself, there's no committing to anything else, other than being non committal to change. Stop complaining about things if you aren't going to do something about it. People will commit to complaining but won't commit to change. Look at your life and determine what you want to improve in your life. We ALL can improve because we should all be growing spiritually, mentally, and emotionally on a day to day basis. Once you decide that you want to commit to yourself, there will be no turning back. You will start seeing a new you and you will absolutely LOVE the new you and find appreciation in the old you.

People will start to see the transformation. Some will "hate on you" but that will let you know you're on the right path. When people nurse misery in their own lives, they create this world of unhappiness and disharmony. So when they see you acting in an unfamiliar way, they figure something is wrong with you because all of the people they associate with are very similar to them... in that DITCH STATUS. They cannot see pass that because they don't want to genuinely see that positive light. For them, it's too difficult, too hard. You just look through that negative spirit as if it was glass and keep climbing the pyramid of self-love and respect. Commit to yourself. It's worth it. You are worth it. You will draw that which you attract to you. You will draw like-minded people to you. You will draw unsolicited supporters of your journey, because your light will shine so much that some people will want the same thing for themselves. Commit to self and act in the now... NOW! Read positive quotes, but also take action. Act in the now! **Now** is the only time that exists.

It's amazing how we as individuals view ourselves in such a negative light. A lot of it has to do with images and shows on TV and in magazines. Or, it may be due to negative behavior that we experience growing up in our household or treatment that we may have received from other kids in elementary school. Whatever the case, the way we see ourselves starts early in life and it becomes a powerful tool in shaping our self-love and self-belief system. I work with a young lady in her early 50's. Every morning I give her a compliment. She knows that I'm testing her each morning but yet she still fails the test day after day. Let me give you an example: I say to her, "Hey young lady! You are looking awesome today!" Now, she wasn't dressed up in a way like some may feel you need to be to get noticed. But her spirit is beautiful and I always let her know that. Well the moment after I compliment her, she looks at herself and says, "Oh, I have gained so much weight…" then, she starts shaking her head. Just when she's about to tell me something else negative about herself, I interject, "STOP THAT! Ah-ah!" She realizes, "I did it again didn't I?" We both laugh about it. I tell her that she needs to learn to "RECEIVE and LEAVE". She asked, "What is that?" I suggested that she learn to accept and RECEIVE a compliment and as soon as a negative thought comes, LEAVE it in the dust. Just say thank you. Accept being beautiful on any given day. It doesn't matter if you are a DIVA or a DON or if you're getting your Kerry Washington or your Denzel Washington on. Just know that you are beautiful. No one gives a compliment to you for you to tear yourself down. Show honor to yourself by accepting the compliment and simply say "Thank you." Be humble, be kind, be gentle, and allow the spirit of love to shine through your being.

Chapter 9
Language Matters

I believe that everything is directly related to your thoughts. If you believe and think that you can do something, then mentally you prepare your body to do what it must, or take action to make it happen. If you believe that you cannot achieve something, your mind shuts down your body, therefore no action is taken, and you are left in the COMFORT ZONE. Henry Ford, founder of Ford Motor Company, stated "Those who think they can and those who think they can't are probably both right." We MUST be our own ally to become successful in our own transformation. It is up to you, not your spouse, mate, best friend, parents, pastor, or anyone else. It is YOU who must do it. One way to condition yourself on your journey is conditioning or changing your language. But you can't only change your language. You must connect with your language. You must totally believe the words that are coming out of your mouth, because it's the only way to speak your reality into existence. Don't hold on to the "old you" if you're trying to create a "new you. I used to be this person that I'm speaking about until one day I decided to actually listen to myself. I decided to record a conversation (with a friend's permission of course) so that I could later go back and listen to myself. I found myself in conservation with a friend who was trying to console me. Every time she would say something positive, I would rip it to pieces defending the negative. The strange thing was, I could hear myself doing this but for some reason I could not control my comments. I was in a Ditch Status. Negativity flooded my thought process. Later that night, I listened to the tape. I was floored by what I was listening to. I couldn't believe that I, someone who tries to be positive as often as possible, was being so negative about my own life. I was going through a depression that lasted seven years after my mother passed away. But I didn't want to be that person on tape anymore. I started reading self-help books, specifically "Acts of Faith" by Iyanla Vanzant. I read a passage that mentioned how we should be more like babies. Babies get up, fall down hard sometimes and get right back up. But adults are afraid to fall. This passage saved my life, so I started changing my language. I started saying and thinking on a different yet very positive level. I started to realize that words and actions are very powerful together. I started speaking things into existence once I truly believed it was achievable. For example, for five years I was a single man doing what single men do. I dated and dated and dated some more. One day, Sept 21, 2004 to be exact, once I got to the level I was reaching for, mentally and emotionally; I truly believed in my heart that I was ready for my wife. Regardless of the past dead end encounters and some very fulfilling friendships, I spoke out loud with conviction... "GOD, I am ready for my wife." This was the same day I wrote my poem "She Could Be My Wife" *(available on iTunes, cdbaby.com and amazon.com)*.

I put out there in the Universe that I was ready for my queen. I had no clue if I already knew her or if she would be a brand new blessing. All I knew was that I was ready to receive her. Almost instantly, I started meeting more quality women; women who were more self-reliant/independent, women who were into the arts, women who truly wanted to be loved. Every week, if not every day, I would say to myself and out loud, that I was ready for my queen. Almost four months later, a young lady who I had been "feeling", who wasn't giving me the time of day, emailed me. She had never emailed me before so I was extremely intrigued with this connection. I called her, we had great conversations, and she really made me laugh. Also, she loved poetry. I was in heaven. August 5th, 2006 we were married and we have a wonderful, loving son that was born in November 2007. This is something big in my life that I truly believe I manifested through thoughts, actions, prayer and meditation. I believed it, I spoke it, and I received it. I believe this is the way our minds should work in accomplishing great things; whether it is love, business, creativity, employment, dreams, or other beautiful things. Sometimes it may take a while, but just hold on and stand in your beliefs. Our language matters, but it must be on the same page as our thoughts. If you believe that you always have bad days and the world is against you, and you speak that negativity out loud, guess what, that will be your experience because you just claimed it. If you think you will always be lonely, and you say "I ain't never gonna find a man/woman", then so be it because you can't see yourself with someone so why would the results be any different? I started realizing that my reality started changing because my thoughts and my language changed. Every day is a beautiful day, so I now speak that into existence daily.

Sometimes things will negatively impact your day, but your situation does not have to define your day. You can choose to speak and think in such a way that it will bring you out of your funk for the day. You must believe.

Chapter 10

Your Greetings Say A lot About You

Around 1995, I worked for a bank card service company. I was a customer service representative assisting customers having issues with their credit card accounts. It wasn't a stressful job and most of the individuals that I worked with were cordial people. I remember going into work each afternoon because I worked the third or evening shift, ready to start off the work day and possibly getting called out of my name from customers angry because I couldn't increase their credit lines or remove finance charges because of a late payment. I've always been the type of person that greets people upon contact, so as I pass co-workers in the office I say "Good Afternoon." From one co-worker I hear "It ain't that good, 'cause I'm sitting here working right now. I could be at home." I would think to myself, "You could be unemployed." Then, on to the next person; we'll call him Bob. "Good afternoon, Bob. How are you?" Bob would respond, "I'm just making it day to day. I'm still here." Now, initially, I'm interacting at a high energy level, but the more I speak with people, the more I start allowing other people's negative aspect of "being here" to diminish my once powerful, strong light. At the time I didn't realize that happiness was a choice. I would think to myself, "These people are depressing." I continued on through my department, still being hurled with negative comments as greetings. I approach someone who we'll call Alex. "How are you today Alex? Good Afternoon." Alex could not even formulate words. He would say "Grrrr" and would not give me enough respect to just look up at me and give me eye contact. "This day is going to be a 'Lucifonic' type of day I see", I thought to myself. (Lucifonic is just my way of saying hellified or extremely stressful and hot in nature). By this time, my energy level has depleted because I let others transfer their negative energy to me. That's a big no-no in my book, but I didn't know any better back then. Finally, right before I would reach my desk, I would walk over to another representative named Blake. Blake is his actual name. You know, like Blake Carrington from the hit prime time show Dynasty. "How are you today, Blake? Good afternoon." Blake would always respond, "I'm doing ABSOLUTELY FANTASTIC. It's a beautiful day. How are you?" Instantly, my energy level would pump back up, as if I was revived from the dead. "I'M AWESOME BLAKE. Thank you", I'd reply. I don't know if Blake ever knew this, but he always made the work day start off great with his greetings and I learned from him that your greeting sets the tone for your interaction through the day.

It is my belief that part of our transformation is not only in the way we look, or how we think, but it also has a great deal to do with the way that we feel and a genuine belief in those feelings. If you don't truly feel good, how can that generate positive energy if you don't truly have it? See, Blake taught me that our greetings are direct responses to how we view our lives. Think about it for a moment. Think about those co-workers that you know that barely speak to you and when they do, they respond as if the world is going to end two minutes after hello. Think about that best friend that constantly has bouts of depression or loneliness connected to not being with a man or woman. When these people respond to your greetings, they are consistently on the downside of life. They are unhappy and it beams through their hello. If you say that "it's just one of those days" or "I'm not that good", the energy that you give with those responses usually stays with you throughout the course of the day. Often, people repeat those responses day after day, never really seeing the positive side of a smile in your voice, because you can't see or feel a smile due to whatever is going on in your life. But when you say "I'm FANTASTIC" or "I'm GREAT" or "It's an awesome day" and you indeed connect with those emotions, your day will consistently stay on that page all day. Try it. Initially, you may feel like you are lying to yourself, until you tap into your happiness and start to build on it. Once you get into the habit of manifesting your moods through your words and emotions, you will feel incredible. It's a positive affirmation and a new way of seeing the world, because the day IS awesome and so are you. If you don't think so, think about those people whose lives may be worse off than yours. Bishop Walter Hawkins' song, "Be Grateful", reminds me of this often.

BE GRATEFUL
by Bishop Walter Hawkins

God has not promised me, sunshine
That's not the way it's goin' to be,
but a little rain

*mixed with God's sunshine.
A little pain
makes me appreciate the good times.*

*Be grateful
Be grateful*

*God desires to feel
your longings.
Every pain that you feel,
He feels them
Just like you,
But He can't afford to make you feel
only good.
Then you can't appreciate
the good times.*

*Be grateful
Be grateful*

*Be grateful
Because there's someone else who's
worse off than you
Be Grateful
Because there's someone else
who'd love to be in your shoes
be grateful
God said it would never
never forsake you
Be Grateful.*

Think about those people who may be less fortunate than you, but still find a reason to smile. I saw something incredible on Oprah's OWN station. There was a man on there (Nick Vujicic) who was born with no arms and no legs. He went through many trials and tribulations but ultimately, he turned what we saw as a handicap into his strength. It was amazing to me. He goes around the country motivating others to be the best they can be. He is a true blessing and the way that he greets and speaks, makes you believe that you are beautiful and that my friend is the point; to feel beautiful and to feel like you are extraordinary. Your greetings introduce others to your greatness; to the peace that is shining through your physical shell. Your greetings and your smile should make the person on the receiving end either curious about the source of your joy, or it should make them want to find out what makes you so joyous. It could possibly rub off on them. Starting today, if you are not already doing this, the next person that you encounter, greet them with strong positive energy. Tell them that you are AWESOME, or FANTASTIC and BLESSED & HIGHLY FAVORED, or something to let them know that you love life and you are living it.

It's quite addicting and it's best to transfer positive energy than to plague another person with negative matter. Be EXTRAORDINARY every day. I now choose to not ask people, "How are you today?" anymore. If your mission in life is to try and save everyone you speak to or with, then this part of this chapter may not be for you. But if you are tired of always giving your energy or allowing it be stolen from you, please continue.

Have you ever had one of those days where you are feeling

extraordinary and your energy is unmatched by any previous feeling? You are feeling awesome. You walk into the office, your job, your home, school, or where ever your destination was, and you say to someone "GOOD MORNING. HOW ARE YOU TODAY?" The way you delivered your greeting was with great passion, conviction, and empowering energy and the person you say it to gives the response "Ugh, it's not a good day today" or "I've seen better days." The human in you naturally will feel compassion for this person so you say "Aw, what's wrong?" The flood gates are now opened and this person releases all of their issues, feelings, energy onto you. They have transferred their pain and strife into your whelm and now your energy that was at 125%, has decreased to about 75%. You naturally try to console them, even though you know you probably can't do anything for them other than listen, because unfortunately, if a person doesn't want to be truly helped, they are not going to hear a thing you have to say. Well, they finally get everything out and they still feel the same way they did when you came in, but now your spirit is down; the transference of energy by Sir Isaac Newton. This could be a moment where your conversation could help someone and this is awesome. It has been my experience that when someone is truly depressed, your words my go in one ear and out the other. They need to vent, but then are not willing to heal or do anything about it. I read a quote once that said "stop complaining about things if you are not willing to change them." I concur. In saying this, ask yourself sincerely, when you ask a person "How are you today?" Do you genuinely want to know? If you do, go to the next chapter. This doesn't concern you. If not, please read on.

I think it's awesome to ask genuinely about the well-being of another human being, but just know, when you do; you are opening up a flood gate that you may not be able to handle. I decided that I'm tired of others stealing my energy away from me. In essence, I'm giving away my power because no one can take my joy away unless I give it to them. I have decided that for now on, I'm NOT asking EVERYONE "How are you today?" anymore.

Instead of using the programmed salutation of asking someone about their feeling and not truly wanting to know, or not readily available to know and discuss, I decided that I will say something like "Good Morning (afternoon or evening). Make it a great day." It actually places the onus on the person to create a joy that no one else can take away from them. Unless it's your personal mission to solve the world's problems, this is all that needs to be said. Now if a person still responds in a negative fashion, it's up to you to decide how to handle it. But it is my belief that your positive energy in your greetings, your smile and your take charge attitude will ultimately wear off on the other person. That same person, who always seems so down, may actually ask you how you do it every day. That's when you have a conversation. It is our job to own our joy, not to give it away. And although to a degree, this method sounds a bit selfish and a little harsh, I enjoy being happy and I am not willing to give that emotion or feeling away to anyone anymore. Let's just chalk this one up as "tough love and self-joy preservation." As stated, when I genuinely want to know, I will ask. We must regulate our own energy and part of the idea of doing that is transferring positive energy more than negative energy. It's so easy to dump negative energy onto the next man or woman, but it is a challenge and a lifestyle to spread love through your energy to all, especially to those who are willing to allow that energy in and not try to nullify it with their self-contained misery. Make sure that you are intentional when you ask someone "How are you doing?" It is essential for a person who is going through transformation to surround themselves with positive people and extraordinary healing.

Chapter 11
Beware of the Buzz Killer

In order to move forward effectively on your journey of transformation, it is essential to surround yourself with other people who think positively and who are trying to move their lives forward. They say if you want to be successful, surround yourself with successful people. If you want to be happy or live with limited stress, surround yourself with happy minimally stressed people. Bottom line is that you cannot transform yourself into a being of positive energy hanging around toxins. People who dwell in negative behaviors and thoughts will throw a monkey wrench in your "Create Me A Better Me" program. This type of energy will bring and keep you down if you allow it to. That is why it is your choice to be happy and forward moving in your life. That is why you must eliminate or at least avoid the Buzz Killer. Buzz Killers enjoy misery, drama, negative thoughts and watching other folks go through similar ills that they may be experiencing. So learn who the buzz killers are in your circle and shield your progress. The Urban Dictionary describes "Buzzkillers" as, "A depressing person; one whose presence tends to darken others' moods, consistently." I didn't create the term, but I have definitely encountered the BIG BK.

What is a Buzz Killer?

A Buzz Killer is an energy parasite that subconsciously or consciously leaches on to positive matter and instantly drains the life out of a wonderful mood or emotion until the subject's high is equivalent to or close to their low. This ties in to the concept of "misery loves company." But let's imagine this further. Notice that I stated that they "subconsciously or consciously leach on to positive matter"? There are many people out there who intentionally set out to destroy your positive mood because they are not happy with self, so they can't fathom why you should be happy when they are not. Others do it unintentionally, which is a much worst situation because they do not realize that their behavior is being that of a self-destructive nature. Both are unfortunate situations but it makes you wonder which Buzz Killer is worse; the intentional, or the subconscious one?

Needless to say, either one is not worth destroying a positive attitude or excitement towards something that's going on in your life that makes you feel terrific. Sometimes, Buzz Killers can come in any form. When I say any form, I'm saying that the BK can be your best friend, co-workers, your parents, teachers, family, your children or even your spouse. So in other words, Buzz Killers are usually, but not limited to, people who are close to you. Because they are close to you, the pain is much stronger and the effect is much greater, because their response to your "good news" usually minimizes the relevance or strength of the announcement.

Once you determine a patterned that has developed in anyone of these people who are close to you, then my suggestion is to make a mental note, and train yourself NOT to tell these individuals about your most glorious moments. All they are going to do is drain the life force out of you and your accomplishments, or whatever your good news may be. AVOID the Buzz Killer!

Buzz Killers are growing more and more each day into an epidemic and I truly believe some people really get excited when they crush someone's positive mood. Have you ever encountered that individual that seems to get annoyed by you because you are smiling all of the time? It's like something is wrong with you because you managed to find a way to smile in a world that offers so much pain, mischief, deceit, and evil energy. You are the bad one because you are smiling. It makes me laugh while shaking my head because this is such backwards behavior. Why would anything be "wrong with you" because you are smiling? "What are you smiling about?" "What's wrong with you?" Seriously? Is this what our society has come to? Are we so desensitized to joy and the feeling of elations that anyone who has peace in their heart is looked upon as an outcast? People will "straight up" dislike you because you are in a good mood or because you found GOD and created a healthier relationship with the creator. People will hate you because you love yourself. You cannot harvest this energy around you. It will stunt your growth, blur your vision, and mentally make you give up on something that is so very achievable. It's easy to start believing in yourself when you don't have corrupted people in your circle. I used corrupted because, just like a virus in your body or on your computer, it can go undetected and cause you or your computer to function less than what your stellar self can do. It slows down like a computer, almost to the point where you just don't even want to turn on your computer. This is how people who are not happy with themselves or their lives behave and they bring that energy around you. AVOID THEM.

In order to effectively transform yourself, you have to surround yourself with similar mentalities. You have to surround yourself with positive thinkers and individuals who believe that happiness is a journey and not a destination, and that a person chooses to be happy. It is a choice.

Buzz Killers are very destructive and stagnant in their ways. They are hurtful to you and anyone who encounters them, but most of all they are destructive to themselves. Avoid the Buzz Killer. Doesn't mean you can't be friends with them, but you best learn what to share with them and what not too. A very wise man, who happens to be my cousin, (Al Caldwell) told me once in conversation, "It's completely selfish for us to want our friends and family to be as excited about something that we have accomplished, because many times our accomplishments remind them of their failures." When he told me this, a light bulb went off in my head and I said, "Ahhhhh". It made sense to me. Now, I'm not sure if these were Al's own philosophies or if he read it somewhere, but the bottom line is that he made me see a light that was never on prior to that. So since then, even though I still get my share of Buzz Killers, because they are everywhere, I now know who to share exciting information with. If your character traits or behaviors consist of constant negative thinking, putting down someone's accomplishments, or giving little to no energy when someone makes themselves vulnerable enough to share it with you, you could possibly be a Buzz Killer.

REPLACE THE BUZZ KILLER with the ENERGY GIVER:

Once you have determined who the Buzz Killers are in your life, replace them with the ENERGY GIVERS. Once again, letting the Energy Giver replace the Buzz Killer's position in your life is not saying get rid of them as a friend. It just means that you have to be careful who you include on your journey, so that the trip is not a bumping self-defeating escapade. An **Energy Giver** polarizes said excitement with positive affirmation of your gifts, acknowledgement of your joy and your passion and encourages you to achieve all that your heart, body, mind and soul has to offer. The Energy Giver makes you feel as if there is a glow surrounding your presence that is magnetic, drawing in positive matter. Keep in mind that you should also be an Energy Giver to yourself. Don't grow dependent on the EG. Be self-motivating, but there's nothing wrong with growing or expanding with the help of the EG. I have several friends that I speak with on a day to day basis that I consider to be

Energy Givers. For example, when I decided to make a healthy food change in my life, I always held conversations with my co-workers Roz, Yvonne and Ramona. They would always give such positive energy and encouragement to achieve and maintain my weight goal. They were also on the same page in terms of trying to make some healthy changes in their own lives. So I always felt encouraged and I always felt like I had a support system. And that's what Energy Givers are… they are support systems designed and strategically placed in your life based on the energy you put into the universe. You attract to you what you are. The same with my cousins Erica, Robert, Renea, Islandia and Tracy; when I wanted to talk about upgrading my wardrobe, they encouraged the fashion, the journey and the mentality behind feeling good by dressing good. I will discuss upgrading our wardrobes in another chapter. Support systems are necessities on your incredible journey. There's no room in your life when you are trying to transform it, for the Buzz Killer.

Remember Buzz Killers can be anyone who intentionally or subconsciously robs you of your joy… or people who you allow to rob you of your joy. Because joy has to be handed over, no one can take it away until you give that person the power to do so.

[_http://www.urbandictionary.com/define.php?term=buzz+killer_]

Stop telling people about your plans for YOU because everyone does not see your vision. Some will be very negative in speech because they do not understand your passion and your drive to create a better you when they have tried and failed.

Chapter 12
Forgiving Yourself

After having long talks with myself, with God, praying and meditating, I realized that I had a lot of anger within me. Anger directly related to acts and events within my family. From the absence of my father during my childhood to the mental abuse and attempted sexual abuse from a cousin, to the way some family members behaved after the passing of my mother, the heartache of losing two children due to miscarriages, etc. This anger was eating away at my soul, thus being poisonous to my health, mind, body and spirit. For many years, I would get instantly irritated or anger would consume me the moment those thoughts emerged. I realized that it was spiritually destroying me. It was like standing outside of myself, watching me do things to myself; but for some reason, I could not stop. Unfortunately, it took the sudden illness and death of my beautiful cousin Kecia (July 17, 2010) that made me re-evaluate what's important in my life. I realized that I cannot just continue roaming through life with a chip on my shoulder. I realize that a person isn't really living if he or she is consumed by anger. I stopped the flow of positive and ongoing energy. Until you clear anger out of your heart, mind and your spirit, there will be no space or placement for happiness, joy, or forgiveness. I learned that in order to live, I must forgive. Not only forgive those people directly involved, or the situation, but forgive myself. It's okay to take ownership over my actions because I may not have caused the anger, but I perpetuated it and allowed it to live within me.

My father came back strong into my life when I was 21. Although we started building a relationship and becoming friends, I believe that I still harvested anger because he wasn't there during my childhood and as a child I didn't see my father trying. Later, I started developing some anger, or perhaps disappointment towards my mother, because I realized that when she and my father weren't on good terms she didn't allow him to see me. But I had to get rid of that anger on both sides, because my father is in my life in a strong way now and my mother was merely trying to deal with the emotions of loving my father beyond their divorce. I get that. My cousin's death made me realize that life is too precious to live in anger or to allow someone in your life that is less than positive. Sometimes you have to let family and some "friends" go, so that you can have the opportunity to flourish and grow. But most importantly, you have to learn to forgive yourself for your role in holding on to the anger. Usually, when we are angry, the other parties involved are living their lives in "their peace" while we boil inside based on the situation. I told myself; no longer will I allow myself to hold on to anger. No longer will I destroy my spirit and allow negative energy as such to overtake who I am. So I forgive myself for not allowing myself to forgive and move on in life. I forgive myself for allowing negative energy to take up space in my heart preventing me to love others and myself properly. I forgive myself for diminishing my power by giving my power away to others.

From now on, I am going to love myself to the fullest so that I can live. Yes, it may be difficult, but difficult isn't impossible and by committing to myself, it is totally achievable.

FORGIVE YOURSELF. True forgiveness is being able to say "Thank you for giving me this or that experience." I am thankful for my past experiences; for they have molded me into the person I am today. To grow spiritually is really about learning to grow or learning more about ourselves.

[Oprah Winfrey Show: The Secret. Lisa Nichols]

Chapter 13

Dress to Feel Good; Dress to Empower

If your clothes could speak for you right now, what message would it say to you and the rest of the world?

It's about dignity. It's about respect. It's about style and class without being an old "Fuddy Duddy". Convey power, influence, authority and confidence. Your clothes do not make you who you are, although many use fashion to "build self-esteem". I believe that dressing to empower yourself with the energy of feeling wonderful every day is a beautiful experience and practice that cannot hurt you. Before you just start buying a new wardrobe, make sure that you have already been working on your self-image, self-esteem, your spirit and your self-love, so that you don't become dependent on the clothing to make you feel good. You don't want your clothes to be the only thing making your self esteem increase. You should feel good about yourself even if you are in a t-shirt and shorts, relaxing on the couch watching television. But the truth of the matter is many of us don't. As Steve Harvey reiterates often, we should "...dress to impress. Best believe that others are watching". But most of all, dress to empower yourself. Dressing to empower yourself will aid you in your already growing self-esteem building. I want to feel like I feel when I purchase a brand new pair of dress shoes. I want to feel like that every day. I dress to feel good, impress, and to empower myself. Once you have worked on your self-esteem diligently, let your spirit be your guide in terms of transforming your outer shell; your clothing and accessories.

On many occasions, you can look at any individual when you are in public, and match their current mood with their current style of dress. The way we dress reflects our current mood and subconsciously plays the role of a visual aid to those who may notice. I decided to put this chapter towards the back of the book because I do not want any of you to get hooked on the concept that the "clothes make the person", because they do not. But one cannot dispute the fact that in most cases, our style of dress is directly connected to our current state of mind, and possibly our image of self. It reminds me of Morpheus in the Matrix when he told Neo that he was looking at his digital self. Morpheus was dressed very well, confident and appeared very powerful. Neo on the other hand was pretty shabby, unsure of himself and full of disbelief. By the time he became "THE ONE", his style of dressed matched his state of mind. By the time you get to this part of the book, it is my hopes that you have been strengthening your mind, body and spirit and this chapter simply poses as an assistant in your life changing journey.

Dressing to empower yourself and your feelings is naturally subjective to individual style. When you decide to enhance your wardrobe, it begins to assist your insides to smile more. It's as if customized theme music instantly turns on and you are moving in slow motion as you walk. That is the feeling that I want to capture every day. Maybe you don't feel that it's necessary to do anything to your wardrobe to create a better you in your universe, but for me, it definitely added a sense of continuous feel good moments. There is nothing better than walking out of your bedroom, into your kitchen and your spouse does a double take on you. That's the feeling I want every day.

I started dressing in suits, shirts and ties every day. Everyone thought I had a job interview daily. A co-worker approached me and said "I see you are dressing up again." I told her, "Well, one day you will be saying 'Ah, you dressed down today'." She said "I don't understand why you dress up every day when you are not required to." I responded "It's not a requirement for me to dress down either." She looked at me, thought about what I said, shook her head in agreement and walked on. People fear what they don't understand, or sometimes get frustrated or irritated when they don't understand the behavioral change of a person. I even had a person tell me that I needed to stop dressing up because I'm making everyone else look bad. Really? Because I make a conscious decision every morning to look in what I consider to be a professional manner, it makes others look bad? That statement may come from a person whose self-esteem has taken a beaten. For me, dressing for work makes me feel more productive, more professional, more confident, more focused, and more goal oriented. When I dress down, it doesn't give me that same sense. The more relaxed looking I am, the more relaxed my work ethic. Now, that's just me. Many people are very productive in dress down attire, because that's what they are used to and that's their comfort level for work. For many people, if the job doesn't require them to dress up, they will not do it (thus the mentality of the young lady I mentioned earlier).

On a professional level, I definitely encourage you to take a look at your wardrobe and upgrade if you can. My suggestion, go to the thrift stores in your area and build up a new you. Or, if you're financially able, go ahead and get your shop on... responsibly. Build on the pride and confidence that you have been working on. People will start asking you what's going on in your life. They will think you have an interview, a hot date, perhaps even a function that you are attending after work. The truth is; you dress up because you want to and it feels good. You will begin to be contagious to a degree or infectious by nature. You may even see others starting to step up their game. The sleepers will start to awaken.

Chapter 14

React by Not Reacting

It's been very challenging not letting certain things or people get to me or to play on my emotional state of being. I have been viewing some of Deepak Chopra's videos on YouTube, listening to Iyanla Vanzant, praying, and tapping within for strength. I have come to realize that the only time I do react in a manner that is outside of my normal self, is when something affects someone I truly care for and love. It usually happens when there is opposition within the conversation and someone (including me) misinterpreted something, or tried to impose what I perceived as being negative energy on me. It seems that when the situation involves someone that I'm not very close to, I tend to ignore the person, almost as if they are invisible. Now, I'm not saying that is the right thing to do, but it really seems peaceful when I am doing it. None the less, I am practicing not to react to the people who hold my heart the nearest.

Creating a better self is not about getting to one place in your life and staying there. It's about continuous evolution of the self; forever growing to be a better human being. With that being said, I am still a work in progress.

I am becoming a better person daily and I am learning that controlling certain aspects of my emotions are challenging. Sometimes I catch myself getting emotional and I think to myself "choose and pick your own battles" or "is it really worth going down this road?" Breathing is very important. I am learning to breathe and leave a situation if I need to, even if it's just to maintain a certain amount of peace. Once again, I am not a perfect being and I don't always get this one right, but I know what to do and where I need to go when reacting off of other people's energy. I have to keep in mind that just because I am having an extraordinary day, it doesn't mean that the next person I encounter is having one as well. Most of the time, those confrontations have nothing to do with me, but I will get the "negative stick to the stomach". Breathe and leave. Inhale, exhale, and leave the room if you must to re-collect your thoughts and energy. Continue having a beautiful day and don't let the moment get the best of you. Your reaction to reacting is simply not reacting at all sometimes. Don't be numb, but know when to breathe and leave. Often we are disappointed by the actions of others, especially when we thought we knew the person. We figuratively keep getting poked in the eye by this energy. Well, the best way to keep from being poked in the eye by a finger, one must stay away from the finger.

I have gotten into the habit of taking a few minutes or sometimes several seconds to breathe with the intentions to relax myself, hourly. Sometimes I will do it at my desk at work, or in my office at home. Breathe in for about five seconds, and then breathe out. Breathe in, and then breathe out, as a sort of hourly meditation. This maintains helping me from getting irritated or aggravated so quickly. Try it yourself to see how calming it can be. This, I have labeled as my Serenity Breathing Technique. It is meant to bring me to or maintain my peaceful state of mind to calm my spirit. Let me know how this works for you.

Chapter 15

The Five Deadly Word Venoms of Self-Defeat

There are many words, accompanied by actions that can delay or desecrate your journey before you get started. In this chapter, let us chime in on five challengers of self-defeat that are usually in your face early on, before you are even clear on your mission. When I was a little child, I used to watch Saturday Morning Kung-Fu movies. There was this film called "The 5 Deadly Venoms". There were five Kung-Fu masters with five different fighting styles; the Snake, the Centipede, the Toad, the Scorpion, and the Lizard. All were extremely deadly. I started thinking about words and actions that could kill your spirit in the same way that these five different Kung-Fu styles could. So I came up with something I call "The Five Deadly Word Venoms of Self-Defeat". These five words are Doubt, Fear, Pessimism, Procrastination and Quit. What's unique about all of these deadly words is that their "fatality moves" all attack the mind.

Deadly Word Venom #1 - Doubt

One of the worst things you can allow into your mind is Doubt. What is doubt? According to Dictionary.com, doubt is "to be uncertain about (something); considered questionable or unlikely; hesitate to believe". Once doubt has seized your mind, it will allow the other four venoms into your mind, which will eventually defeat you and any dreams that you may have if you let it. Doubt will make you question yourself even when you know that you are qualified or capable of achieving and accomplishing a goal. To be honest, I faced this foe head on when I started writing this book. The thoughts of doubt came into my mind with questions like "Who am I to write a book about transformation?", "I'm just a regular person. Who is going to listen to me?", and the self-doubting statement "I don't know if I can do this. I'm still working on myself." Doubt is the greatest "Jedi Mind Trick" ever. We can defeat doubt. I would pray and meditate to seek my answer. Then, out of nowhere it would seem that I would receive random e-mails from people I didn't know personally, folks on Facebook, Google+ or Twitter; or even someone who I may have published in the SpokenVizions Magazine, encouraging me to continue doing what I'm doing. Some even suggested that because of the work that I do, it has made them a better artist and gave them the courage to move forward with their mission. So the trick is to be resilient to negative energy and forces trying to stop you in your tracks. Believe in yourself and others will follow in that same belief. Eliminate doubt. Put it out of your house.

Deadly Word Venom #2 – Fear

What is fear? According to Dictionary.com it is "a distressing emotion around by impending danger, evil, pain, etc, whether the threat is real or imagined; the feeling or condition of being afraid." If I'm trying to be cool, I would say that fear is the "Number One Stunta". It stunts our growth as creative beings. It stunts our growth as people evolving in our own space. It keeps us in place as would a slave master, or an overseer. It stunts our growth in general. After doubt has laced our minds with disbelief of self, fear will capitalize on the moment. Fear will make you freeze in place, mentally and physically. You can become so afraid of moving forward or so afraid of doing something that you love, that you literally will not move forward and you will stay stuck in a non-progressive time frame, because you allowed doubt and fear to tag team you out of your dreams.

Deadly Word Venom #3 - Pessimism

What is pessimism? According to dictionary.com, pessimism is "the tendency to see, anticipate, or emphasize only bad or undesirable outcomes, results or conditions, problems, etc." Pessimism will definitely catapult you into a "Buzz Killing Frenzy". There's nothing worse than having a conversation with a person who only pulls out negative conversations or subjects. I believe that such a person was conditioned by experiences and consistent let downs in life, therefore, they can never see the cup as being half full because in their eyes there is no water in the cup at all. Being a pessimist will destroy the transformation process before you start your journey because the pessimist has already determined that self transformation will not work, so putting forth an effort to success has already been abandoned; pessimism.

Deadly Word Venom #4 - Procrastinate

What does it mean to procrastinate? To procrastinate is to defer action: delay: to put off till another day or time, defer/delay (dictionary.com). This action verb really doesn't have much action at all. I believe that for many, procrastination takes place because there is a belief of failure brewing deeply within. We delay action towards a goal because we do not believe succeeding will follow our endeavors, so our thoughts are held hostage by doubt, fear and pessimism. I believe this will disappear once we fill our minds and hearts with hope, faith and love for self.

Dead Word Venom #5 - Quit

What does it mean to quit? According to dictionary.com to quit is: a) to stop, cease, or discontinue: b) to depart from; leave: [and] c) to give up or resign, to let go; relinquish. Many people quit situations because it's easier to just give up on something than it is to weather the storm and stick it out. Again, I believe this action is directly related to the other four word venoms. A person who believes in their self will go the distance even if he or she will not come out on top. They believe that giving their all is an accomplishment in itself. Someone who quits all of the time probably has it embedded in their mind that they will not complete the task anyway. They give up on themselves based on doubt and fear, which is the tag team defeating your journey to happiness and transformation.

These venomous words and actions will keep any person stagnant in a world of defeat. It's best to work on the elimination of the power of these words. Changing the way you think in general is the catalyst to creating a better you. Once we eliminate the negative thought patterns that have been holding each of us back, the positive will take over and spread throughout our entire lifestyle. The key is to believe that you are worthy... period. We are worthy of having a great life, a beautiful home, a successful career, a wonderful love interest or spouse, money, etc. Then, as Mary Mary stated in one of their songs; "Go get it. Go get your blessings." That is truly the path I am on.

[Dictionary.com, LLC. (Lexico Publishing, LLC, 1995). Copyright © 2013.]

Chapter 16
Set the Tone for the Week

When you say "Good morning" to someone, do you actually mean that the morning is good or are you just giving a programmed response or greeting that is not connected to your true emotions? If it's a programmed response, then we need to delete that program, re-write it, and then reboot. It is extremely important for us to take control of the tone of our mornings and maintain it or enhance it throughout the course of the day. In doing this, it also sets the tone for the week. I believe that any day you can open your eyes, breathe and think, is a wonderful day. It's another day that you can make a difference in this world, or your world for that matter. We should show appreciation each morning for the ability to function and for being in good health; thankful for having a healthy mind, a healthy spirit. I decided to attach an adjective to every day of the week to set the tone for that day. Now, this is not a new method and I'm sure you have seen others do this, but I'm implementing this as a daily ritual. I wanted something that would stick in my mind just like "hump day" has become the day most working folks look forward to.

We all know people who start the morning off on a bad note. Some people hate that Monday has come around again for us to start the week over. Most people hate Mondays so much, that they start the day off waiting for Friday. Every day is an important day and we have the power to make each day extraordinary, filled with good deeds, and we can also fill the atmosphere with positive vibes. Why destroy your day before it even gets started with negative comments about the start of the week? What if you're like me, and you work every single day of the week? I do not know Mondays like the average person. There are no "weekends" for me because for the last three years, with the exception of three weekends, I have worked every weekend. I decided to make every day a beautiful day. I'm simply thankful for being here and I want to show and give thanks to God for allowing me to see another day. So I have compiled a list of adjectives to go along with each day of the week. Try these out and see how they work for you. One thing I have learned is that you have to mean it when you say it. You have to create it by saying it and acting upon it. I've even added a greeting to my twitter page that I post almost every morning: "Good morning brilliant people. Have a magnificent morning, an awesome afternoon and an extraordinary evening. Live life in wonderful peace." I have gotten a lot of DMs (direct messages) on twitter thanking me for my energy early in the morning. Now try it. It truly makes a difference in life and impacts others.

Spectacular Sunday

Spectacular: Marked by or given to an impressive, large-scale display. Dramatically daring or thrilling. Sunday has always been a day of rejoicing and renewing of one's spirit. It's also the beginning of a new week for most people, so I believe in starting the week off on a very high note.

Monumental Monday
Monumental: Exceptionally great, as in quantity, quality, extent, or degree; a monumental work. Of historical or enduring significance. In fine arts, having the quality of being larger than life; of heroic scale. Instead of huffing and puffing about it being Monday again, I decided to make Monday my flagship to do or at least continue amazing things. This could be the start of a legendary week.

Thankful Tuesday
We should be grateful for all that we have and know. Although I am truly thankful daily, designing a day at the start of the week to be grateful for everything is a wonderful way to start up the week and build up momentum to a beautiful one.

Worthy Wednesday
Worthy: Having adequate or great merit, character or value; deserving. A person of eminent worth, merit or position. We are definitely worthy of all good things that happen to us. We are worthy of a better, healthier and happier life. Knowing our self worth is essential for our self growth, so acknowledge and accept it.

Triumphant Thursday
Triumphant: Having achieved victory or success; victorious; successful. Claim the victory of maintaining

a positive and forward moving life. Every day is a victory but it's up to us to decide what that victory is. For me, it is a day to reflect on accomplishments I have achieved and to set forth new tasks/goals to complete. I am victorious.

Fearless Friday
Fearless: Without fear, bold or brave; intrepid. Be bold going into your weekend. Never stop moving forward. This is not a day to rest, but a day for progress. For many of us, another work week is completed. For others, the weekend is time for business, creating and implementing ideas and travel. We can do anything if we align our thoughts and action. We have made it through another work week. We can do anything.

Sensational Saturday
Sensational: Producing or designed to produce a startling effect, strong reaction, intense interest, etc. Extraordinarily good; conspicuously excellent phenomenal. We are the managers of our own happiness. Stop depending on others to create happiness for us. If we keep our energy at a high level, others will want to know what's so sensational about today.

> *"We are all Super Heroes. Many of us just haven't tapped into our powers yet. Many of us just don't believe that we are powerful."*
> *-Floyd Boykin Jr.*

[(Excerpts of definitions from Dictionary.com). Dictionary.com, LLC. (Lexico Publishing, LLC, 1995). Copyright © 2013.]

Chapter 17
Life is Full of Possibilities

There is no better feeling than waking up each morning knowing that today you will continue to make a difference. It could be in your own life or someone else's life, but you will make a difference. That is very empowering in itself. Will Smith, the mega superstar actor and hip hop artist, has been quoted as saying "If you are not making someone else's life better, then you are wasting your time. Your life will become better by making other lives better."

When people who have a certain chain of thought that was created based on their experiences, and they deem themselves as being cursed, or everything negatively always happens to them. They are speaking or willing that life into existence. They are claiming that life, so why would it be any different than what they think it would be. Within their own minds, they have created this planet, or this universe of negative conception and it rules their existence because they allowed it to be as such. And when a positive thinker comes about and tries to explain this to the negative thinker, who will look at the positive thinker in such a way, it almost appears that the positive thinker is crazy and tainted. But isn't it crazy to claim a curse or put a negative claim on your life that it will always be this way? When a person says "this is who I am and that is the way I'm gonna always be", that's a cop out and a growth prohibitor. If you're going to claim something, claim a better life and believe it, then be ready to receive the blessings or the energy that the universe will deliver to you. The Creator will allow your vision in your head to come true. You just have to go and get it and make it happen.

> *"Life is full of possibilities, and I... I matter.*
> *I can make a difference. I believe in me.*
> *And although times get dark*
> *The sun is always shining*
> *My mission may not be clear to all,*
> *But as long as I'm clear, the mission is possible."*
> *- Floyd Boykin Jr.*

Here is the chorus or hook from one of my favorite inspirational groups, Mary Mary. It has helped to purge and recollect my thoughts and purpose on many occasions:

> *"Take my heart and make me over*
> *Lord because I love you*
> *You're my soul my life my*
> *Source of everything the*
> *Very reason why I*
> *Live each day in love I*
> *Live each day in love with*
> *You forever"*
> *- Excerpt from the song "What Is This"*
> *by Mary Mary*

So in closing, this has been a book written to express my journey in creating a better me, to create a better future for myself, as well as for my family. It has been a long road, but no road is too long when you are receiving what you need to grow. Take the time to commit to self, for when you commit to what your truth should be, that is when you will know and find love within self.

Thank you so much for taking the time to experience my expedition and if anything in this book has helped to make your life or thought process a little better, then I'm on the right path. I have my son recite to me every morning before starting his school day, "Have fun, be respectful and learn something amazing." Be brilliant in your way and be extraordinary. ☮

Recommended Readings

Other books by Floyd Boykin Jr.

Poetry Books

Poetic Bliss With Lyrical Rhythms, *(SpokenVizions Entertainment Group, LLC. 2000)*
ISBN: 0-9773834-0-7

Bare Essence: The Soul Of Me, *(SpokenVizions Entertainment Group, LLC. 2004)*
ISBN: 0-9773834-1-5

Waiting To Dance With Her Spirit, *(SpokenVizions Entertainment Group, LLC. 2007)*
ISBN: 0-9773834-3-1

Recommended Musical Project

Other projects by Floyd Boykin Jr.
Musical Recordings

Project L.I.F.E. (Learning Information For Existence)*(Floyd Boykin Jr., sponsored by the Lupus Foundation of America, Missouri Chapter. © 1999)*

Planet Liberation, *(SpokenVizions Entertainment Group, LLC. © 2002)*

EKLIPSE, *(SpokenVizions Entertainment Group, LLC. © 2004)*

EARTHOLOGY, *(SpokenVizions Entertainment Group, LLC, © 2009. Available on iTunes, CDBABY.com and Amazon.com)*

W.A.R. on RedMoon7 *(SpokenVizions Entertainment Group, LLC. © 2011. Available on iTunes, CDBABY.com and Amazon.com)*

Create Me A Better Me is an Empowerment Movement.

Testimonies are always beautiful to hear when you are on your path of happiness and transformation. It truly helps to motivate others along their way to transforming and creating a better person. Write to Floyd Boykin Jr. and tell him about your successful journey into self. We would love to have your permission to publish your testimonies, so please grant us your permission to do so. Allow others to see it is beautiful to take a chance on your self and let love shine through.

E-mail us at <u>ABetterMe@spokenvizions.com</u>

Visit Floyd at his website at <u>www.floydboykinjr.com</u> to view these testimonies.

Index

Acceptance and complacency, 1-2,
- Stagnant in complacency, 4

Acknowledgement, 7, 50

AEE Method, 7
- Acknowledge, Empowerment, Excitement, 7
- Acknowledge, 11

Affirmation, 3

Al Caldwell, 49

Anger, 53-54,

Awesomeness, 10,
- Awesome, 40
- Looking awesome today, 33
- I Awesome⋯, 39

Be Grateful, 40-41
- Bishop Walter Hawkins

Beautiful, 33

Believe, 26-28, 34-35, 64, 66, 68, 70-71, 73

Betray, 4
- Betray our hearts, ourselves, 4

Better you, 9, 13

Blessing(s), 9

breathe and leave, 61,
- breathing, 61
- Serenity Breathing Technique, 62
- Breathe and think, 68

Buzz Killer, 46-51
- Buzz Killing Frenzy, 65

Change, 1, 4, 9 -12, 15, 31, 51
- Changing the way you think, 14
- It will never change, 21
- Change the way you think, 23
- Changing your language, 34

Character, 25, 28, 70
- Attractive character, 27
- Enhance Character, 25

Childhood, 53
Clearing a Path, 16
Clutter, Cluttered, 17-19
Comfort Zone, 34
Commit to Yourself, 31-32, 53, 74
Complain, 1-3
Confident, 27, 58,
- With confidence and humility, 27
- confidence, 56, 59,
Courage, 28, 64,
Create, created, 2, 13, 17, 23, 25, 27, 29-30, 32, 34, 46, 52, 58, 60, 71,72, 74
Creating a better being (me), 14, 74
- create a Permanent emotional tenant, 2
- Create space 3, 5
- Creativity – 36
- Creative being, 65
- Create a better you, 2
- Create Me A Better Me Affirmation, 13
Deepak Chopra, 60
Depressed,10
- People are depressing, 39
- bouts of depression, 40
Ditch Status, 20, 32, 35
- Break the chain of the "DS" , 22
Dressed up, 33,
- dress, 57-59
- dressing good, 51
- dress to empower, 56-57
- dress to impress, 56
Emotional, 4, 16, 19, 35, 47, 61,
Empowerment, 7-8
- Empower you, 8,
- Empower us, 11
- Empower, 29, 57,
Energy, 11, 17-18, 26-28, 39-40, 43-44, 46, 48-49, 51, 53-54, 59, 61, 64, 69, 71, 73,
- Energy parasite, 47
- Evil Energy, 48
- ENERGY GIVER, 50-51
Enhance, 7, 57,
- Enhance yourself, 7
Excitement, 7-8
- Excited, 11

Extraordinary, 19, 26, 30, 43, 45, 61, 69, 74
Faith, 7, 13, 18, 66
Fear, 6, 63 (see Five Deadly Word Venoms)
Feng Shui, 17, 19
- Karen Kingston, 17,19
Five Deadly Word Venoms of Self-Defeat, 63
- The Five Deadly Venoms, 63
- Doubt, 63, 66,
- Fear, 15, 1, 64 , 65 (number one stunta) , 66
- Pessimism, 63, 65,
- Procrastination, 63, 66,
- Quit, 63, 66,
Flood gates, 43-44
Focus, 26-27
Forgiving, 53
- Forgive/forgiveness, 53
- Forgive myself, 54-55,
Get Naked, 4-5
God, 8,11, 18, 25-26, 35, 40-41, 48, 53, 69
- The universe, 8, 36, 72-73
- The Creator, 18, 48, 73,
- The Higher Power, 18
- Lord, 73
Gratitude
- Journal 15
Greatness – 16
Greetings – 38-39
- I' m Fantastic, 39-40
- Tone – 16:1
Grow – 6, Growth, 73-74
Happiness, 14, 26, 38, 40, 53, 66, 71,
- Happy,19, 47
- Happiness is a journey, 14, 49
Health, 14, 53
- Healthier eating, 11
- Healthy mental state, 25
- Mental health, 26
- Healthy Mind, Healthy Spirit, 68
Help, 20
Henry Ford, (Ford Motor Company), 34
Honest, 28
Humility, 27, 30

Image of self, 57,
Ignorance, 6
Illness, 1
- Emotionally, spiritually and physically, 1, 21,
Inna Rae - Introduction
Integrity, 28
Iyanla Vanzant, 35, 60
Journey, 8-9, 14, 25-26, 29, 34,
51, 63, 74
Knowledge, 29
Language, 10, 34, 36
Law Of Attraction, 8
- Attract situations, 21,
Life, 9-10, 17-18, 25, 27, 35-36, 51, 53-54,
59, 67, 70, 72-74
Love, 25-26, 28, 31-33, 60, 67, 74
Lucifonic, 39
LUPUS, 10
Manifest, 1
Mary Mary, Introduction, 67, 73
Meditation, 25, 36, 61
- Prayers and meditations, 36
- meditating, 53
- meditate, 64
Michael Beckwith, Dr., 9
- Grateful, 9
Morality, 28
Morpheus, 57
Motivational, 6
Negative, 18-19, 23, 32-37
38-39, 52, 54, 60-61, 64-65, 72
- Negative people, thoughts, 19-20
- Negative words about yourself, 23
- Negative stick to the stomach, 61,
Neo. 57
Nick Vujicic, 42
Oprah Winfrey, 23, 42
Organize, 27
Pastor Joel Osteen, 20, 23
- The Power of I AM, 23
- I Am..., 23-24
Peace, 2, 19, 44, 48, 54

Physical, 16, 19
Poems, 18
Positive, 35, 39, 44-45, 47, 53-54,
62, 67, 72,
 - Think positively, 46
 - positive affirmation, 50
Powerful, 12, 32, 35, 38, 71,
 - Power(s), 19, 51, 54, 67, 71
 - 12 Power Words, 25
 - Giving away my power, 44
Programmed Response, 68
Purpose, 4, 25-26
 - What is my purpose?, 25
React, 60-61
Receive and Leave, 33
Re-evaluate, 4
RE-Factor, 14
Renewing one' s Spirit, 69
RE-Shape, 15
Reshape, 4
Resilient, 28
Respect, 28, 39,
Self. 6, 31, 60, 70
 - Self- esteem, 26, 56-58
 - Self-defeat, 63
Set Tone for the Week, 68
 - Spectacular Sunday, 69
 - Monumental Monday, 70, Monday(s) – 68-70
 - Thankful Tuesday, 70
 - Worthy Wednesday, 70
 - Triumphant Thursday, 70
 - Fearless Friday, 71
 - Sensational Saturday, 71
Sir Isaac Newton, 43
Smile, Smiling, 19
Spirit, 2, 4, 30, 33, 53-54, 56-57, 62
 - Spiritual landlords, 2
 - Spiritual baggage (emotional/mental), 4, 9

- Vulnerable spiritual self, 5
- Spiritual Enlightenment, 5
- Spiritual or religious belief, 13
- RE-condition my spirit, 15
- Spiritual, 19
- Spiritually and morally grounded, 28
- Spiritual Beliefs, 31
- Growing spiritually, mentally, and emotionally, 32, 55
- spiritually destroying me, 53

Steve Harvey, 56,
Super Heroes, 12
Thankful, 55
Thoughts, 6, 34, 61
- Healing your thoughts, 6

Transformation, 3, 8, 17, 32, 34, 39, 45-46, 64-65
- Transform, 7
- Transformation of self, 11, 25
- Transforming thoughts, 4
- Transforming YOU, 19
- Transform the outside, 5
- Transform ourselves, 5
- Three Keys to Transformation, 6-7
  Transform it, 51

Transition, 7
Trust, 26-27
Victory, 70-71
Vision, 26, 29, 48, 52
Vision Board, 17, 26-27
- An organizational tool, 17

Will Smith, 72
Words, 9, 25, 27-28, 34, 39, 67
- Venomous words, 67

Create Me A Better Me: A Conversation About Self-Transformation

www.floydboykinjr.com
www.spokenvizions.com

www.ingramcontent.com/pod-product-compliance
Lightning Source LLC
Chambersburg PA
CBHW060358050426
42449CB00009B/1801